Dietrich Bonhoeffer

Who Am I?

Poetic Insights on Personal Identity

Augsburg Books

MINNEAPOLIS

Dietrich Bonhoeffer

*A Brief Summary
of His Life*

Dietrich Bonhoeffer was born on February 4, 1906, in Breslau, Germany. His father, Karl, was Professor of Neurology and Psychiatry, and his mother, Paula, was a committed Christian, who devoted herself to running the household and raising their eight children.

Dietrich was a sensible, gifted, and clever child. Along with his siblings—Susanne, Sabine, Christine, Ursula, Klaus, Walter, and Karl-Friedrich—he received religious instruction from his mother from the time he was very young. When Dietrich was six years old, the Bonhoeffer family moved to Berlin. There he attended prep school *(Gymnasium)*, subsequently studying theology at the University of Berlin and receiving his second doctorate at the age of twenty-four.

A Brief Su

In addition to his vocation as a pastor, he next studied in New York and later in Berlin. Important trips to Italy and New York greatly affected his personality and attitude. But in 1933 his life was fundamentally changed when Adolf Hitler seized power. From then on he engaged passionately in the church's opposition to Hitler's regime. Resistance was forbidden by law, but for Bonhoeffer it stood within the context of love for those who had to endure severe injustice.

In October 1933 Bonhoeffer went to London, where he served as a pastor for two years. While he was there, he often reported on the actions of the National Socialists (Nazis) in Germany. Later, on the Danish island of Fanö, he gave many notable speeches on peace. And due to his untiring engagement in further political activities as well as connections with Jews, he drew even more scrutiny from the Nazi regime.

Back again in Germany, he undertook the leadership of the illegal seminary in Finkenwalde near Stettin, which was forcibly closed shortly thereafter by the police. Bonhoeffer pursued his work with the underground, and finally in 1940 he was officially banned from teaching, preaching, or publishing.

Bonhoeffer took a second trip to America in the summer of 1939, but he broke it off after six weeks. While he knew that it had become dangerous for him in Germany, it was impossible for him to leave his family and friends alone in those difficult times. Up until then, Bonhoeffer's resistance had all been within the context of the church; but after his return it became political.

When he was thirty-seven, Bonhoeffer met the eighteen-year-old Maria von Wedemeyer, to whom he became engaged in January 1943. But they were never married, as Bonhoeffer's conspiratorial work was discovered. The Gestapo arrested him on April 5, 1943. This began his incarceration in Tegel Prison. After an unsuccessful assassination attempt on Adolf Hitler, he was moved to the main Gestapo prison on Prinz-Albert-Strasse in Berlin.

In February 1945, Bonhoeffer was taken to Buchenwald concentration camp and finally to the Flossenbürg concentration camp. It was there, on April 9, 1945 (shortly before the end of World War II), that he was condemned and executed on Hitler's order, together with other resistance fighters.

The notes and letters from this period of imprisonment, which had to be smuggled out, were published after the war as *Letters and Papers from Prison*. They are examples of decency, courage, and intelligence, attracting worldwide recognition, and that is the reason that today Dietrich Bonhoeffer is one of the most widely read theologians.

Bonhoeffer's two best-known poems—"Powers of Good" and "Who Am I?"—testify particularly to the tension between depression and inner strength and are part of these papers. The letters between Bonhoeffer and his fiancée are collected in the book *Love Letters from Cell 92*. For Bonhoeffer, his fiancée's letters, which were brought to his cell, brought him "inexpressible joy."

Who Am I?

Who am I? They often tell me
I emerge from my cell
serene and cheerful and poised,
like a noble from his manor.

Who am I? They often tell me
I speak with my guards
freely, friendly, and clear,
as though I were the one in charge.

Who am I? They also tell me
I bear days of misfortune
with composure, smiling and regal,
like one accustomed to victory.

Am I really what others say of me?
Or am I only what I know of myself?
Disquieted, yearning, sick, caged like a bird,
fighting for breath itself, as at the hands of a strangler,
craving colors, flowers, birdsong,
thirsting for kind words, human closeness,
shaking with rage at tyranny, the pettiest offense,
tossed about in anticipation of great events,
helpless in worry for friends endless distances away,
tired, with nothing left for praying, thinking, working,
weary and ready to take leave of it all?

Who am I? This one or the other?
Am I one today and another tomorrow?
Am I both at the same time? Before others a hypocrite
and in my own eyes a contemptibly self-pitying weakling?
Or does what remains in me resemble a defeated army,
retreating in disorder before victory already won?

Who am I? It mocks me, this lonely probing of mine.
Whoever I am, thou knowest me; O God, I am thine!

Who am I? *They often tell me*
I emerge from my cell
serene and cheerful and poised,
like a noble from his manor.

Morning's first light, pale and gray,
slips through my window;
A light, warm summer breeze passes over my brow.
"Summer day!" I breathe, "Beautiful summer day!"
What might it bring me, pray?

Then outside I hear steps, quick and restrained,
at my door suddenly contained.
Hot and cold blood-flow:
I know, oh, I know!

Who am I? *They often tell me*
I speak with my guards
freely, friendly, and clear,
as though I were the one in charge.

 Obedience follows blindly,
freedom has open eyes.
Obedience acts without asking questions,
freedom asks about the meaning.
Obedience has tied hands,
freedom is creative.
In rendering obedience human beings
observe God's Decalogue.
In exercising freedom they create
new decalogues.
In responsibility both obedience and freedom
become real.

Who am I? *They also tell me*
I bear days of misfortune
with composure, smiling and regal,
like one accustomed to victory.

 In its essence, optimism is not
an outlook on the present situation.
Rather, it is a life-force,
the power of hope when others give up,
the power to hold one's head high
when everything appears to be falling apart,
the power to endure setbacks,
the power that never gives
the future over to one's opponent
but lays claim to it.

Am I really
what others say of me?

 Wishes to which we cling too tightly
can easily take from us
some of what we should and could be.
Wishes we repeatedly overcome
for the sake of the present task
make us—paradoxically—richer.

Or am I only

what I know of myself?

I am alone.
There is no one
to whom I might pour out my heart.
So I pour it out to myself
and to the God
to whom I cry out.
It is good
to pour out one's heart
in loneliness
rather than to let care
eat away at us.

This is a time when there's so much to say that silence is the only real answer. One's heart is so full of good, peaceful, grateful thoughts and knows that it's so safe from all dangers and tribulations that it would like to share some of what it has undeservedly been given.

Excerpted from Dietrich Bonhoeffer's letter to his fiancée, Christmas Eve, 1943

Disquieted, *yearning, sick,*
caged like a bird,
fighting for breath itself,
as at the hands of a strangler.

Lord God,
misery has come over me.
My afflictions are about to crush me;
I don't know which way to turn.
God, be gracious and help me.
Give me strength to bear what you send.
Do not let fear
rule over me.

craving colors, flowers,
birdsong,
thirsting for kind words,
human closeness,

It is infinitely easier
to suffer in obedience to a human command
than in the freedom of the most personal act
of responsibility.
It is infinitely easier
to suffer in community than alone.
It is infinitely easier
to suffer publicly and with honor
than at the margins in disgrace.
It is infinitely easier
to suffer through putting one's bodily life at stake
than one's spirit.

What I'd ceased to think possible has happened—indeed, has fallen to my lot. It has been granted me to love again and be loved, to rejoice in that love for the first time, and to hope for its fulfillment. That, Maria, is why I thank you.

Excerpted from Dietrich Bonhoeffer's letter to his fiancée, May 29, 1944

shaking with rage at tyranny,

the pettiest offense,

tossed about in anticipation

of great events,

There are times
in which everything real
is so bewildering
and so distressing
that any direct word
seems to us to destroy the mystery of God,
that we wish to speak and listen
to others speak
of the last things only obliquely.
Everything we are able to say
about our faith
appears then so flat and empty
in contrast to the reality
we are actually experiencing,
behind which we believe
is an inexpressible mystery.

helpless in worry for friends
endless distances away,
tired, with nothing left for praying,
thinking, working,

Fear is the net
spread by the evil one,
in which we can easily become entangled
and brought to a fall.
If we are afraid, we have already fallen in.

But I have often found that the quieter my surroundings, the more
vividly I sense my connection with you all. It's as if, in solitude, the
soul develops organs of which we're hardly aware in everyday life.
So I haven't for an instant felt lonely and forlorn.

Excerpted from Dietrich Bonhoeffer's letter to his fiancée, December 19, 1944

weary and ready

to take leave of it all?

 We are no longer able to hate death so much;
we have traced in its features something of kindness
and have almost made peace with it.
Deep down we seem to feel
that we already belong to death,
that each new day is a miracle.

Who am I? *This one or the other?*

 I often ask myself
who I really am:
the one always cringing in disgust,
going to pieces
at these hideous experiences here,
or the one who whips himself
into shape,
who on the outside
(and even to himself)
appears calm, cheerful, serene, superior,
and lets himself be applauded for this charade—
or is it real?

Am I one today

and another tomorrow?

Am I both at the same time?

I lapse into brooding,
plunge into the depth of darkness.
You, O Night, full of sacrilege and evils,
reveal yourself to me!
Why do you prey upon our patience—and how long?

Silence, deep and sustained;
then I hear the night inclining toward me:
I am not dark, guilt alone is dark!

*B*efore others *a hypocrite*

and in my own eyes

a contemptibly self-pitying weakling?

Far away or close by,
in good fortune or ill,
each friend in the other discerns
the faithful helper
into freedom,
into humanity.

*It's a cloudy, rainy day outside, a perfect accompaniment to my
fruitless wait for the situation to resolve itself. But let us never forget
how much we have to be thankful for, and how much good we expe-
rience even so; I have only to think of you, and all the little shadows
on my soul disperse.*

Excerpted from Dietrich Bonhoeffer's letter to his fiancée, August 12, 1943

Or does what remains in me

resemble a defeated army,

retreating in disorder

before victory already won?

 It is one of the most astonishing experiences—
and one of the most incontrovertible as well—
that evil, often in a surprisingly short period,
proves itself to be stupid and impractical.

Who am I? *It mocks me, this lonely probing of mine.*

 It is the advantage and the nature of the strong
that they pose the great questions of decision
and are able to take a clear stand
in relation to them.
The weak must always decide
between alternatives
not of their own making.

Your picture, with which I have to be content for weeks on end, is hanging in front of me, but now I hear your voice once more. And your laugh—even when we laugh, we're a trifle sad, aren't we? I see your eyes, I feel your hand. Everything is absolutely real again. How can I thank you for everything? I can't, I can only tell you that all is well when you're with me.

Excerpted from Dietrich Bonhoeffer's letter to his fiancée, November 10, 1943

Whoever I am, *thou knowest me;*

In me it is dark, but with You is light.
I am lonely, but You do not abandon me.
I am faint-hearted, but from You comes my help.
I am anxious, but with You is peace.
In me is bitterness, but with You is patience.
I do not understand Your ways, but You know
the right way for me to go.

O **God,** *I am thine!*

By powers of goodness wondrously well-sheltered,
We trust, beholding all that comes our way.
God is with us each evening and each morning,
And comes afresh to us on each new day.

Source Credits:

Pages 19, 23, 27, 35, 39 excerpts at bottom of page from: *Love Letters from Cell 92: The Correspondence Between Dietrich Bonhoeffer and Maria von Wedemeyer 1943-45*, edited by Ruth-Alice von Bismarck and Ullrich Kabitz. Postscript by Eberhard Bethge. Translated by John Brownjohn. Copyright © 1993 CH; Beck'sche Verlagsbuchhandlung, 1994 HarperCollins Publishers, Ltd. Used by permission of Zondervan Publishing House.

All other excerpts from: *Dietrich Bonhoeffer Werke* by Dietrich Bonhoeffer. 17 vols. Edited by Eberhard Bethge et al. Munich and Gütersloh: Chr. Kaiser/Gütersloher Verlagshaus, 1986–99. English translation: *Dietrich Bonhoeffer Works*. 17 vols. Wayne Whitson Floyd Jr., General Editor. Minneapolis: Fortress Press, 1996–.

Page 13 from DBW 6: *Ethik*. Edited by Ilse Tödt, Heinz Eduard Tödt, Ernst Feil, and Clifford Green. Munich: Chr. Kaiser, 1992; Gütersloh: Chr. Kaiser/Gütersloher Verlagshaus, 2d ed. 1998, page 288. English translation: *Ethics*. Edited by Clifford J. Green. Translated by Reinhard Krauss, Charles C. West, and Douglas W. Stott. Minneapolis: Fortress Press, 2004, page 288.

"Who Am I?" poem and pages 11, 15, 17, 21, 23, 29, 31, 33, 35, 37, 39, 41, 43 from DBW 8: *Widerstand und Ergebung*. Edited by Christian Gremmels, Eberhard Bethge, and Renate Bethge, with Ilse Tödt. Gütersloh: Chr. Kaiser/Gütersloher Verlagshaus, 1998, pages 513f, 522, 36, 358f, 208, 35, 37, 235, 520, 589, 29, 551, 204f, 608. English translation: *Letters and Papers from Prison*. Edited by Wayne Whitson Floyd Jr. Translated by H. Martin Rumscheidt, Lisa Dahill, and Reinhard Krauss. Minneapolis: Fortress Press, forthcoming, page numbers not yet available.

Page 27 from DBW 13: *London 1933-1935*. Edited by Hans Goedeking, Martin Heimbucher, and Hans-Walter Schleicher. Gütersloh: Chr. Kaiser/Gütersloher Verlagshaus, 1994, page 345. English translation: *London: 1933-1935*. Edited by Keith Clements. Translated by Isabel Best. Minneapolis: Fortress Press, forthcoming, page numbers not yet available.

Page 19 from DBW 14: *Illegale Theologenausbildung. Finkenwalde 1935-1937*. Edited by Otto Dudzus and Jürgen Henkys, with the assistance of Sabine Bobert-Stützel, Dirk Schultz, and Ilse Tödt. Gütersloh: Chr. Kaiser/Gütersloher Verlagshaus, 1996, page 854. English translation: *Theological Education at Finkenwalde: 1935-1937*. Edited by Gaylon Barker. Translated by Douglas W. Stott. Minneapolis: Fortress Press, forthcoming, page numbers not yet available.

Page 25 from DBW 16: *Konspiration und Haft 1940–1945*. Edited by Jørgen Glenthøj, Ulrich Kabitz, and Wolf Krötke. Gütersloh: Chr. Kaiser/Gütersloher Verlagshaus, 1996, page 194f. English translation: *Conspiracy and Imprisonment: 1940-1945*. Edited by Mark Brocker. Translated by Lisa Dahill. Minneapolis: Fortress Press, forthcoming, page numbers not yet available.

Photo Credits:

Pages 10, 28: © Karlheinz Klubescheidt, Rheda-Wiedenbrück; Page 12: © Pieter Jos van Limbergen, Köln; Page 14: © Wolfgang Ehn, Mittenwald; Pages 18, 40, 42: © Gerd Weissing, Nürnberg; Page 20: © Fridmar Damm, Köln; Page 24: Reinhard Kemmether, Nürnberg; Page 26: © Werner Heidt, Mannheim; Page 32: © Corbis, Düsseldorf; Page 36: © Peter Santor, Karlsruhe. All other photos: Archiv Gütersloher Verlagshaus GmbH, Gütersloh

ISBN 0-8066-5116-4

First English-language edition published by Augsburg Books in 2005.

Original German edition © Gütersloher Verlagshaus GmbH, Gütersloh 2004.

English-translation copyright © 2005 Augsburg Fortress, Publishers. All rights reserved.

Reproduction: MohnMedia, Mohndruck GmbH, Gütersloh
Printing and Binding: Těsínská Tiskárna, Česky Těšín

Printed in Czech Republic

09   08   07   06   05   1   2   3   4   5   6   7   8   9   10